ACCELERATE

AN 8 WEEK DEVOTIONAL DESIGNED TO PROPEL
A STUDENT'S WALK WITH GOD

WRITTEN BY **JACOB OUELLETTE**

Accelerate Devotional
— *a daily guide to propel a student's walk
with God.*

Copyright © 2012 Jacob Ouellette
ALL RIGHTS RESERVED

Published by PCG Legacy, a division of
Pilot Communications Group, Inc.
(www.thepublishinghub.com)

www.ignited.org

ISBN: 978-1-936417-56-8

Printed in the United States of America

DEDICATION

I want to dedicate this book to the incredible students of Ignited. It is such an honor to work with you to impact thousands of teens. You have truly accelerated the Gospel in our area and around the world.

TABLE OF CONTENTS

INTRODUCTION

I am so pumped about your desire to grow in God. I know, for a fact, that if you seek God, you will find Him and that is exactly what this book is designed to help you accomplish. It's time to know personally how real God is for your own life.

There is no reason that you cannot have a thriving relationship with the One who created you! It is time for you to discover the heart of God, how to please Him and what He wants you to accomplish.

The bottom-line is this: It is time to step on the spiritual gas pedal and accelerate your life in God.

HOW THIS WORKS

First, "Read" through the opening scripture & the thought of the day.

Second, "Read" the verse from your own Bible when you are prompted to read.

Third, "Think" deep about the question and write your answer in the book.

Fourth, "Act" out the closing challenge.

Lastly, "Close" in prayer. If you will commit to this over the next eight weeks, I guarantee that you will accelerate your faith in Christ!

THE ULTIMATE LIFE

A thief is only there to steal and kill and destroy. I came so they can have real and eternal life, more and better life than they ever dreamed of.
— John 10:10 (Message)

Think back to a time when someone gave you something that you really wanted. It could be clothes, a video game system, or something for your birthday.

Do you remember how excited you were?

Now, even if you multiply that by 10, it doesn't even begin to explain how much God wants to bless you. God's heart is to bless your socks off. He wants to truly give you the ultimate life.

Some of you may feel that you are far from that now, but a person who is committed to God will begin to watch God's love and blessing dump on their lives in ways they never dreamed possible.

If you want to be a part of the ultimate life, then strap on your seat belt and start accelerating today!

ACCELERATE TODAY

Read — Psalm 37:4-5

Think — What do these verses mean to you?

Act — Make a decision today to live a life fully committed to God.

BELIEVE

God loved the world so much that he gave his one and only Son so that whoever believes in him may not be lost, but have eternal life.
— John 3:16 (NCV)

You cannot see the wind, but I think we would all agree that it is there. You can feel the effects of the wind. The same is true when you choose to believe in Christ. You will see and feel the effects of God and His love in your life.

This is so vital to the foundation of your faith in God.

You must truly and totally believe in God, believe that He exists, believe that He died for you and rose from the dead, and believe He wants to bless you. If you are still having a hard time with this concept and want to know how to grow your belief, you must seek Him.

God is not trying to play hide and seek with you. The Bible says, *"draw unto me (God) and I will draw near to you"* (James 4:8a). Go after God, and watch your belief and your faith Grow!

ACCELERATE TODAY

Read — Matthew 7:7-8

Think — How will you apply these verses to your life?

Act — Make it a lifelong goal to grow in your belief of God.

CONFESS

If you confess with your mouth the Lord Jesus and believe in your heart that God has raised Him from the dead, you will be saved.
— Romans 10:9 (NKJV)

I heard a story where a father had to take his daughter to school late because of a doctor's appointment. It was school policy that he go with her to sign her in at the attendance office.

As they were walking down the hallway, the daughter tried to walk a little faster than her dad so no one would know that they were together. Every time he called her, she ignored him. Many times people act like that with God.

They may believe in Him, but the last thing they would ever do is tell others that they have given their life to God.

This breaks God's heart just as it would any father.

There is more to your relationship with God than just believing in Him. God wants you to say something about it. He wants you to let people know your life has changed and why.

The Bible says you confess with your mouth and you believe in your heart. This is a two-part process. You believe in your heart and you do something about it ... confess with your mouth.

ACCELERATE TODAY

Read — Luke 12:8-9

Think — What are some things you can work on to be bold in confessing and telling others about God?

Act — Tell somebody about the greatest decision you have ever made ... giving your life to God.

UNDERSTAND

In reply Jesus declared, "I tell you the truth, no one can see the kingdom of God unless he is born again."
— John 3:3 (NIV)

Spiderman, also known as Peter Parker, was an average guy until he had a radical, life-changing experience. His life was forever changed the day he became Spiderman.

That is the key when we give our lives 100% to God. We are different and we should act different.

You see, when you give your heart to Christ, the Bible says you are "Born Again." You are changed on the inside. You don't look or feel different, but you are now committed to God instead of yourself. You must understand the change that happened on the inside. God has come to live in your heart. He has come to have a personal relationship with you.

You must know and believe that this made a difference in you.

ACCELERATE TODAY

Read — 2 Corinthians 5:14-17

Think — Do you believe this? What does this verse mean to you?

Act — Understand that God has changed your heart and begin living differently.

BAPTISM

Peter said to them, "Change your hearts and lives and be baptized, each one of you, in the name of Jesus Christ for the forgiveness of your sins. And you will receive the gift of the Holy Spirit." — Acts 2:38 (NCV)

You must be baptized. If you have given your life to God, then He wants you to be baptized.

What is baptism? It is simply you telling the world that you are committed to God. When you go under the water, you are signifying that your old ways are now dead. When you are brought out of the water, it signifies a new life in Christ.

Old things are now passed away, and you are different and ready to show the world.

Baptism is an honorable thing that pleases God.

Think about it: You are so proud of your walk with God that you want to tell the world and be obedient to God's Word in Baptism. This is a powerful and important step in living for and obeying God.

Sign up at your church, and invite your whole family to take part in this special moment in your life.

ACCELERATE TODAY

Read — Acts 2:40-42

Think — Have you been baptized? What is stopping you from being baptized?

Act — If you have not been baptized, talk to a church leader this week!

GOD'S PROUD

The master answered, "You did well. You are a good and loyal servant. Because you were loyal with small things, I will let you care for much greater things. Come and share my joy with me." — Matthew 25:21 (NCV)

Recently, I had the opportunity to speak on Sunday morning in front of the whole church for the first time. I was nervous, sweating, and shaking.

There was a packed crowd and my whole family was there.

I remember stepping up to the pulpit and everyone staring at me waiting to see what I was going to say. I took three deep breaths, stepped up, and gave it all that I had.

As soon as I was finished, my parents ran up to me and gave me the biggest hug. They both had tears in their eyes.

They kept telling me how proud they were and how they were letting everyone know that I was their son.

When you give God your all and commit every area of your life to Him, God is so happy and all of heaven cheers. He and all the angels in heaven are proud of you. They basically throw a party just because of you.

God loves you so much, and there is nothing that makes him more proud than when you give your life and heart totally to Him. If you haven't made a decision to give God your life, then turn to page 123 and commit your life to Him now.

ACCELERATE TODAY

Read — Luke 15:1-7

Think — Write down some thoughts on these scriptures.

Act — All of Heaven is cheering because of you! Continue to make God proud.

CHANGE TODAY

Choose for yourselves this day whom you will serve ... But as for me and my house, we will serve the Lord.
— Joshua 24:15 (NKJV)

If you are going to accelerate your relationship with God, then you need to change some things that you are doing now. If you just gave your life to God, then you have many areas that need to change in order to be pleasing to God.

Even if you have been following God for a long time, there is always something that needs to go.

That's what this whole thing is about: accelerating your walk with God and getting closer to Him. The truth is there are things in our lives that keep us from getting closer to God and those things are sin. You must want to be pleasing to God and desire to change more than you want to keep sin in your life.

You must search your life and begin to deal with these areas if you are going to accelerate your life towards God.

When I gave my life to God in 9th grade, I had some bad habits already formed. I had no idea how I was going to stop drinking, swearing, lying, and being disrespectful. I remember praying and saying, "God I want to change and do what's right but I have no idea how ... help."

I felt God encouraged me to focus on only one day at a time. When you think of it this way, your habits become beatable. All you've got to do is take it one day at a time, one decision at a time, and watch your old habits go right out the window.

ACCELERATE TODAY

Read — James 1:21-27

Think — What are five areas that you need to change to be more pleasing to God?

Act — Begin today to honor God in every way for the rest of your life.

FOOD

Give us this day our daily bread.
— Matthew 6:11 (NKJV)

More than 925,000,000 people suffer from hunger (www.bread.org). That's about three times the population of the USA. Hunger kills 16,000 children every day, or over 6 million each year. Three out of four who die are younger than five years old.

Can you remember a time when you have been absolutely starving?

Maybe there has been a time when you haven't eaten all day and your body is screaming for food! God made us the same way spiritually.

We have got to have a consistent intake of spiritual food (the Bible), or we begin to starve and deprive our spirits of its greatest need — food from God.

We must daily put spiritual food in us, if we are going to thrive as a Christian.

ACCELERATE TODAY

Read — Matthew 4:1-4

Think — How will you incorporate spiritual food in your life everyday?

Act — Do not starve yourself from spiritual food!

GROW

But grow in the grace and knowledge of our Lord and Savior Jesus Christ. Glory be to Him now and forever! Amen. — 2 Peter 3:18 (NCV)

Imagine a young married couple having a baby. Due to their inexperience with children, they forget to feed the baby, hold it, care for it, or change its diapers when needed. How many of you know that this baby would not be very healthy?

The parents only care for the baby when they feel like it and, then they wonder why it's not growing up to be a healthy person.

Spiritually there are a few things that are vital for the growth of our spiritual life. One of them is a consistent intake of God's Word.

We will not grow into a strong human, if we are deprived of growth. When you begin to feed on God's Word, your spirit begins to grow, and you begin to become spiritually healthy. If you don't want to be a spiritual weakling, then grab your Bible and begin to grow!

ACCELERATE TODAY

Read — Psalm 27:7-8

Think — When is the best time in your day to seek God by reading the Bible/eating spiritually?

Act — Set aside time everyday to read God's Word—the ultimate food!

POWER

God's word is alive and working and is sharper than a double-edged sword. It cuts all the way into us, where the soul and the spirit are joined, to the center of our joints and bones. And it judges the thoughts and feelings in our hearts.
— Hebrews 4:12 (NCV)

Have you ever plugged something into the wall only to find out that the outlet is not working? So you go through all of the effort checking every plug in the room.

Frustrated, you are searching the whole house for a working electrical outlet. Our life can be like that spiritually.

We can be searching every possible outlet for something powerful and something that will make a difference in our lives.

It's not until we plug into God's Word that we will see the lights turn on and God's power come in our life.

The Bible is not a useless plug, but rather a powerful outlet that is always ready and waiting for you to plug in.

ACCELERATE TODAY

Read — Ephesians 1:15-23

Think — What areas in your life do you need God's Power ... His help?

Act — If you want God's life-changing power, then plug in today!

ADVICE

Ask, and God will give to you. Search, and you will find. Knock, and the door will open for you.
— Matthew 7:7 (NCV)

Young children ask up to 400 questions per day. That is a ton of questions.

All of us have lots of questions about many things in our lives.

Who should I date?
Where should I go to college?
How do I act towards my unfair parents?
What is this God stuff all about?

These are all great questions and every single answer is found in God's Word. God's Word will give you insight and advice into situations that you would never have gained if you hadn't turned to God.

He will show you the type of people who are good to marry and who are not. He gives you advice about His will for your life and future, how to respond to your parents, how to work hard, and how to have a great family when you get older.

We must read God's Word to tap into His insight and advice. Think about it, who in their right mind wouldn't want God's advice on something?

ACCELERATE TODAY

Read — James 1:5-8

Think — What are some issues you need to turn to God about?

Act — Do you want perfect advice? Read God's Word and you will find it!

PAIN

He said to them, "My heart is full of sorrow, to the point of death. Stay here and watch with me."
— Matthew 26:38 (NCV)

I can remember when I was asked to officiate my first funeral. The lady who passed away left a husband, five children, and 14 grandchildren. Needless to say, there were many people crying and dealing with a great deal of pain due to the death.

You may have gone through something very painful or maybe you are going through something now.

The key is for you to turn to God and you will be comforted.

You will be given hope and a future. You must turn to God and His Word for Him to bless you and fill your life with His love and comfort.

In Psalm 34:18 the Bible says, "The Lord is near to those who have a broken heart, and saves such as have a contrite spirit."

ACCELERATE TODAY

Read — Psalm 23

Think — How can this bring help in painful times?

Act — If you are in pain, turn to God who can help.

GOD'S VOICE

My sheep listen to my voice; I know them, and they follow me.
— John 10:27 (NCV)

What if you wrote the love of your life a note, but he/she didn't want to take the time to read it? In fact, the person you gave the letter to didn't think it would be worth reading.

How would that make you feel?

What if the love of your life took the time to write down thoughts and feelings towards you and you never opened it to find out what it said?

Many people complain because they say they never hear God speak. The truth is, God took all this time to write you a letter (the Bible) and tell you many things that would benefit your life greatly.

All you have to do is open the Bible and start reading; God's voice will speak to you. The Bible is the main way you can hear the voice of God. It is available anytime you pick it up and begin reading.

ACCELERATE TODAY

Read — John 10:22-30

Think — What can you gain from this scripture?

Act — God will speak to you everyday ... open His letter!

CORRECTION

The Lord disciplines those he loves, and he punishes everyone he accepts as his child.
— Hebrews 12:6 (NCV)

There are many things in God's Word that may confront you. There may be some things that you are doing that the Bible speaks against.

We must take this as a warning and see God's correction and then make the change.

You've heard the story of the kid who wanted to play out in the road. His father told him to stay out of the road with a stern warning. The kid refused the father's correction and responded with kicking and screaming, furious at the thought that his dad would limit his play area.

The kid would never know that if he had heeded the warning, he would have saved his life.

Sometimes we don't understand why God tells us not to do certain things, but let me assure you the best thing you can do is heed God's warning and trust His Word: the Bible!

ACCELERATE TODAY

Read — Hebrews 12:3-11

Think — What are some areas in your life that God is trying to correct?

Act — We must learn to heed God's correction. It can only help us and never hurt us!

IDENTIFY

"This is how you should pray. 'Our Father in heaven, may your name be honored. May your kingdom come. May what you want to happen be done on earth as it is done in heaven. Give us today our daily bread. Forgive us our sins, just as we also have forgiven those who sin against us. Keep us from falling into sin when we are tempted. Save us from the evil one.'" — Matthew 6:9-13 (NIRV)

This is the model prayer that Jesus recited when he was teaching the world how to pray.

There are some extremely important things that we can note from this historic prayer.

The very first thing that Jesus does is identify who He is praying to. He says, "Our father in heaven ..."

He is not just calling to a higher being or just a form of God. Jesus is praying to the one true God in heaven. This is vital for you to grasp, if you are going to accelerate in your walk with God. You must pray to God, the God of the Bible, our Lord Jesus Christ.

Some of the people you know may believe that you must pray, but they have no idea who they are actually praying to. The first step to an effective prayer is identifying God as the One you are praying to.

ACCELERATE TODAY

Read — Matthew 21:18-22

Think — What are some things or areas in your life that you need to start believing God for in prayer?

Act — 1. Write those things down.
2. Begin to believe God for those things daily.
3. Memorize verse 22.

THANKS

Pray like this ... may your name be honored. — Matthew 6:9 (NIRV)

In dealing with the model prayer, the second thing that is said is, "... may your name be honored." This is an act of praise or thanks.

It's important to note because after you have identified God as the One you are praying to, then you should begin to praise Him.

Begin to tell Him how great He is and how honored you are to know Him.

Think about it, if someone came to you all the time and all they ever said was what they want from you, it would get a little annoying.

God has set up this prayer model to show us how to approach Him.

So, instead of just going into prayer instantly spouting off your needs, you must begin to share your heart with Him and express your love to Him.

Prayer is more about God than it is about you, and it's important that you pray with this understanding.

ACCELERATE TODAY

Read — Psalm 8:1-9

Think — What are some things you can say to honor God in prayer?

Act — In every prayer you pray, let God know you honor Him.

GOD'S WILL

Pray like this ... May your Kingdom come. May what you want to happen be done on earth as it is done in heaven. — Matthew 6:10 (NIRV)

God is the creator of the entire universe, and He created you as well.

Don't you think He knows what is best for your life?

One of our natural tendencies in prayer is for us to tell God what and how we want things done. God wants us to be more concerned with His will and what He wants to do in our lives.

When we are going to God in prayer over something in our lives that we need help on (which is every day), we must seek what He wants and not come with our own agendas.

Listen to the heart behind these words, "May your kingdom come soon. May your will be done ..." This is the cry of a loyal soldier who desires nothing more than to please his commander.

This is how our prayers must sound, "God, I want your way over mine. Whatever you want is what I want."

ACCELERATE TODAY

Read — Matthew 26:36-39 (Jesus' prayer before the cross)

Think — What can you learn about Jesus in this passage that you can apply to your life?

Act — Commit to pray what God wants, not what you want. Commit to His will even if it is the tough thing to do.

ASK

Pray like this ... Give us today our daily bread. — Matthew 6:11 (NIRV)

Going into my 10th-grade year, I prepared for football like no one else on my team. I remember working out two hours a day. I would work on heavy weights and intense sprints.

The season finally came and the coach decided to start a different person in the spot that I had earned. Heart broken, I went to the coach after practice and told him how hard I had worked and asked him to give me a chance in the game.

He saw the passion in my eyes and decided to give me that chance. From the next game on, I earned my position and ended up being the captain of the football team my Senior year. It all started with a question.

Listen, you are talking to God. He can do absolutely anything!

The Bible says in James, "You have not because you ask not."

Here is how you have success in prayer: When you ask God according to His will, it will be done.

For example, you cannot ask Him if you can rob a bank because you would like some money. Stealing is a sin, and sinning is not His will. It is when we ask God and it does not go against His nature that He will answer our prayers.

ACCELERATE TODAY

Read — James 4:1-3

Think — Why do you think that people ask for what they want instead of what God wants? What is wrong with this?

Act — Things to ask for: God's will to be done, for you to grow in your relationship with God, for people you know to come to Christ, that you will make right choices to honor God today, that you will grow in wisdom, etc.

FORGIVE

Pray like this ... forgive us our sins, just as we also have forgiven those who sin against us. — Matthew 6:12 (NIRV)

If we are going to accelerate our lives for God, then we have got to come to grips with the concept of forgiveness.

Forgiveness is a two-step process. Number one: God wants us to ask forgiveness for the things that we have done wrong. Not just a little "I'm sorry," but a true and total repentance.

You must turn completely away from those sins, never to go there again.

Number two: God wants us to forgive other people for what they have done wrong to us. This is one of the devil's greatest attacks on humanity. He wants you to hold on to bitterness and hard feelings toward people.

This will weigh you down and consume your mind, if you don't let go of the hurtful things of the past.

It is more painful and damaging for you to hold on to the hurt caused by another person than the actual act. Don't let the devil make your past more painful than it already is ... let go!

If we are going to live victorious lives, then we must ask God for forgiveness and deal with our sins. We must let go of our painful past by forgiving those who have hurt us.

ACCELERATE TODAY

Read — Matthew 6:14-15

Think — What are some things you need to ask God to forgive you for? Who are some people that you need to forgive?

Act — Do the right thing by forgiving and asking for forgiveness. Don't wait any longer. Remember, you will be forgiven when you forgive.

RELATIONSHIPS

Pray like this ... forgive us our sins, just as we also have forgiven those who sin against us. — Matthew 6:12 (NIRV)

This is the same verse as yesterday, but we are going to take a different angle on it today.

Being forgiven and forgiving others is a big part of what? ... Relationships.

Relationships are what we deal with almost 24/7. People have the most enjoyable and most troubled times with people or relationships.

This is another area we must continuously pray about. We can pray that we find friends who love and honor God. We can pray that God will impact our family. We can pray that God will bring the right spouse into our life at the right time. We can pray for those who don't like us.

We can pray that we would respond better to those in our life. We can simply pray for all those we love and know.

These are just a few of the thousands of types of prayers we can pray for those we have relationships with.

ACCELERATE TODAY

Read — Romans 12:9-12

Think — Who are some people in your life you would like to pray for?

Act — Pray for the people who are in your world everyday.

PRIORITIES

(a) And don't let us yield to temptation, but deliver us from the evil one.
(b) For Yours is the kingdom and the power and the glory forever. Amen.
— Matthew 6:13 (a-NLT) (b-NKJV)

In part (b) of this verse, there is a list given (kingdom, power, glory) that indicates priorities. We must have right priorities in our lives.

There is a huge difference between a teenager who "believes in God" and a teen who makes God their #1 priority.

God never said, "It's ok, you can put me on the back shelf. I don't need to be a priority in your life."

God says, "Love the Lord with all your heart, soul, mind and strength" (Mark 12:30). This again indicates priority.

If you are going to accelerate in God, you must put Him first. Everything else in your life must be second to your daily relationship with Him. Pray that God will help you put Him first in your life.

ACCELERATE TODAY

Read — Mark 8:34-38

Think — How does this speak to you concerning your priorities?

Act — Put God first in your life and exercise this priority daily.

SHAPED

He who walks with wise men will be wise, but the companion of fools will be destroyed.
— Proverbs 13:20 (NKJV)

You have heard the statement, "garbage in, garbage out."

This is true.

I have got to be a little honest with you; one of my weaknesses is fast food. I am over the top with Whoppers, Big Macs, Double Bacon Classics, and a pile of hot salty fries smothered in ketchup with a Coke so big it wears you out to just hold it.

If I am putting this in my body every day, you can only conclude it would damage my arteries, heart, weight, and overall health.

Friends are similar to the foods we eat. If we choose friends who influence us in ways that are displeasing to God, it is only a matter of time before it begins to affect our lives in a destructive way.

The truth is, we are shaped by our friends!

ACCELERATE TODAY

Read — 1 Samuel 20:1-4

Think — Was Jonathan a good friend; and if so, why?

Act — Surround yourself with people who will push you towards God.

DRAG

Some friends may ruin you, but a real friend will be more loyal than a brother. — Proverbs 18:24 (NCV)

A top fuel dragster can go a quarter mile in under four seconds, and they can reach over 300 mph before you were able to read this sentence. That is smoking fast!

Even with the great power and aerodynamics of this dragster, it cannot even come close to its top speed when its parachute is deployed.

This may describe some of you.

You want to go after God with everything you've got.

You read your Bible, pray, and tell others about God, but your parachute is out dragging you down. Some of your friends are telling you to slow down with all this God stuff and relax.

They might be cracking jokes about your love for God or church. You are trying to go after God, and they are trying to get you to put on the breaks. Friends, do what God wants you to do.

You must care more about God than you do your friends that are trying to slow you down.

ACCELERATE TODAY

Read — Proverbs 17:9

Think — List some people you feel drag you away from doing what is right.

Act — Begin to spend more time with those who push you in God and less time with those who don't.

IRON

As iron sharpens iron, so a man sharpens the countenance of his friend. — Proverbs 27:17 (NKJV)

Many years ago, if you wanted to sharpen your sword to get ready for battle, you had to use other iron or metal.

It would be the last mistake of your life to take a dull sword into battle.

The Bible says that good, godly friends can be a sharpener in your life. They will influence you in a way that makes you more of a man or woman of God.

Think of surrounding yourself with people who will sharpen your life and make you better simply by just being around them.

Remember, this does not come easy. Finding the right friends is a challenge at times. None the less, it is one of the most important things you could do in life.

Search high and low until you surround yourself with iron that will sharpen you and push you closer to God.

ACCELERATE TODAY

Read — Matthew 7:7-8

Think — What do these verses tell you about finding friends?

Act — I want to challenge you to look until you find those friends. Ask until you get your prayers answered.

PALL BEARERS

The way of a fool is right in his own eyes, but he who heeds counsel is wise. — Proverbs 12:15 (NKJV)

A great man of God once said to me, "You must get six men around you who can be your pall bearers." A pall bearer is one who carries a casket.

At the time, I thought he was kind of weird, but now I understand what he was saying.

It is important that we find a few friends (pall bearers) who can lift us up when we get down.

When things are going rough in our lives, we need dependable people we can turn to for comfort, love, and advice.

Begin to think about your own life. In your life right now, what are your closest friends like?

Are they the ones you want standing next to you when you are broken and desperate for godly advice, love, and comfort?

Maybe you need to begin to bring other friends (pall bearers) into your life who will pick you up when you are down.

ACCELERATE TODAY

Read — Luke 10:30-37

Think — What are some things that you can learn from these verses?

Act — Find a handful of good friends who are dependable and can help you when you are down.

BE

Do to others what you want them to do to you. — Matthew 7:12 (a) (NCV)

I have heard it said so many times, "I don't have any friends." One of the first things I tell them is that to have friends, you must be one.

You cannot expect friends to fall out of the sky and into your life.

If you want more friends, then start being friendly to more people.

No one wants to be friends with the person who just sits in the corner of the lunch room and doesn't say anything. You must be proactive.

You have got to be the person who makes the effort. The longer you are the first to be friendly, the more friends you'll have.

If you would get up and be nice, kind, courteous, and fun then you would start to make friends. It doesn't matter who you are; if you want more friends, then you need to be friendly.

ACCELERATE TODAY

Read — 1 John 3:16-19

Think — What are some qualities that you would want in a friend?

Act — Begin to act towards others in the way that you would like them to act toward you.

DREAM PUSHERS

Do you not know that friendship with the world is enmity with God? Whoever therefore wants to be a friend of the world makes himself an enemy of God. — James 4:4 (NKJV)

This scripture above is a powerful statement. The truth is you can be one of two types of people: you can be a dream crusher or a dream pusher.

Your friends need people around them who will believe in them and push them toward greatness.

This is essential to being a great friend. Jesus was the greatest dream pusher. He encouraged people and believed that they could go after their dreams and fulfill God's plan for their lives.

What kind of person are you?

Are you one to discourage people, be sarcastic, and rip into them? Or, are you one who lifts them up, inspires them, and motivates them to be all they can be in God?

The choice is yours. Are you going to be a dream crusher or dream pusher?

ACCELERATE TODAY

Read — Psalm 119:63 & Proverbs 22:11

Think — What are some things you need to change to become a dream pusher? Who are some people you know who are dream pushers?

Act — Be a dream pusher yourself, and hang around those who can lift you to your highest potential!

INFLUENCES

Don't make friends with quick-tempered people or spend time with those who have bad tempers.
— Proverbs 22:24 (NCV)

Have you ever been at a restaurant and someone said to you, "Man, you have got to try this. It is amazing!" So you take his or her word for it and almost puke when you taste it.

This is an example of a person who influenced you.

I define *influence* as the power to produce an effect, whether indirectly or through someone else. The truth is, an influencer can be anyone around you.

People influence our thoughts, attitudes, morals, beliefs, and tons of other things.

It is vital that you surround yourself with people who will influence you in good things toward God. If not, it may be a lot more serious than gagging over a gross meal your buddy told you to try.

The pain from bad influencers can harm you for years. The bottom line is choose wisely the people that you allow close to you!

ACCELERATE TODAY

Read — Genesis 37:16-20

Think — How did Joseph's brothers influence each other? Do you think it is important to have people of good influence in your life?

Act — Put people around you who will influence you to do the right things and grow in God.

CLARITY

Everyday I will bless You, and I will praise Your name forever and ever.
— Psalm 145:2 (NKJV)

Worship is two fold, First, worship is your lifestyle, and worship is the way you live.

To God, living right is pleasing Him.

If someone is hurting in school, then extend yourself and encourage them. Other forms of this lifestyle of worship are helping your mom with the dishes, setting the example for your brothers and sisters, remaining sexually pure until you're married, and taking a stand for God in school.

Secondly, worship is a time to connect with God at church. At church there is a part of the service that most churches usually call a "worship or praise" service. Songs are played and people express their devotion to God. The band is not up there to look and sound good. This is a time specifically created for you to express your love to God. This is a time when you can tell God how much you love Him and how much He means to you through the singing of songs.

Both aspects of worship are important to God and are of great significance if you are going to accelerate towards God. The key is not to do one or the other, but you must incorporate both in your life.

ACCELERATE TODAY

Read — Psalm 95:1-5

Think — Do you feel that you worship God in both ways as described above? And if so, how?

Act — Make worship a part of who you are.

LIFESTYLE

But let all those who worship you rejoice and be glad. Let those who love your salvation always say, 'Praise the greatness of God.'
— Psalm 70:4 (NCV)

It wasn't long ago that I got married and yes it absolutely rocks! Hannah is my dream come true!

In our marriage, I must live a consistent and moral lifestyle. If I were to do the right things only when she was around, the relationship would never work, and it would fall apart.

If I took the liberty to do anything, such as having some girlfriends on the side, I would be not only dishonoring God, but I would be dead meat.

The truth is worship must be a way of life.

It must be something you do 24/7. You must exalt God in everything you do. If not, your relationship with God will soon be non-existent.

It's time we live a lifestyle that is pleasing to God at all times. This is true worship.

ACCELERATE TODAY

Read — Psalm 34:1-4

Think — What are some simple but practical things you can do that will be an act of worship to God?

Act — Live out a lifestyle of worship that is pleasing to God everyday.

DEVOTIONS

Let the saints be joyful in glory; let them sing aloud on their beds.
— Psalm 149:5 (NKJV)

Devotions are a time that we set aside every day to connect with God. Many people find that when they get out of bed in the morning, it is the best time to jumpstart their day by connecting with God.

During devotions, we pray and read the Bible looking for ways to hear and understand God.

I want to challenge you to bring worship into your devotions. I am not saying invite the youth band over to your house, but rather tell God how much you love him. Take time to worship and exalt God. Express from your heart the most honoring things you can think of and tell them to God.

This can really bring life to your devotions. God deserves our praise and our worship every day.

ACCELERATE TODAY

Read — Psalm 92:1-2

Think — How often does God deserve your praise?

Act — Begin to incorporate worship into your daily devotions.

LIFT

*Thus I will bless You while I live; I will
lift up my hands in Your name.*
— Psalm 63:4 (NKJV)

The little boy who just learned how to run finds
himself stumbling on the sidewalk that runs
parallel to his house. His right leg has caught the
back of his left leg and has sent him into a helpless fall to the rough concrete.

As he tries to pick himself up off the ground, his
knees and elbows dripping with blood, he begins
to cry for his dad.

The father comes running out to find his son
with arms open wide and tears streaming down
his face. The dad picks him up and soon after that
the boy stops crying.

We have all been there.

**After we have been hurt, our arms reach
upwards in our cry for help.**

Worship is the same way. We lift our hands not only because He is God and He deserves it, but also because we need Him. We need a lift.

God hears our cry and comes to comfort us.

ACCELERATE TODAY

Read — Psalm 141:2 & 1 Timothy 2:8

Think — Do you think God is embarrassed when you lift your hands at church? In what ways do you feel you need a lift from God?

Act — Get beyond your feelings and reach out to God. Lift your hands to God this week during worship at church.

NEW SONG

*Oh, sing to the Lord a new song! Sing
to the Lord, all the earth.*
— Psalm 96:1 (NKJV)

If I were to give you a compliment, you would probably feel pretty good. But, if I gave the same compliment to you every day, after a while it would get old ... real old.

In our lifestyle of worship, God wants us to praise Him.

He wants us to put a new song in our hearts, or in other words, He wants us to get creative in the way we praise Him.

Think about being real with God, being honest with Him and talking to Him like you actually believe in Him.

When you praise Him, come up with something new to say, something that is relevant in your life, something that will bless Him everyday.

ACCELERATE TODAY

Read — Psalm 96:1-13

Think — Make a list of some new things you can praise him for.

Act — Praise Him everyday!

WORSHIP THROUGH LOVE

Beloved, let us love one another, for love is of God; and everyone who loves is born of God and knows God. He who does not love does not know God, for God is love.
— 1 John 4:7-8 (NKJV)

As we have been reading, we realize that worship is a lifestyle. If the way you live can be an act of worship and love is pleasing to God, then loving people is an act of worship.

God's heart is exactly the opposite of the devil, which is loneliness, hate, abuse, suicide, and much more.

God's central theme is love. So many people are struggling with things that the devil can steal from them or lie to them about. People need to simply experience God's true love.

Guess what — you are one of the ways that people can experience His love. When you respond selflessly to others and love on them the way God would want, you are worshipping.

Go show God's heart to this desperate world and worship away!!!

ACCELERATE TODAY

Read — 1 Corinthians 13:1-8

Think — List some things you can do to express worship to God in the form of love to others.

Act — Love people just like 1 Corinthians 13:4-8 says.

SONGS

Praise the Lord! It is good to sing praises to our God; it is good and pleasant to praise him.
— Psalm 147:1 (NCV)

Some of you may ask, "Why do we sing songs at church? Why is that considered worship?".

That's a great question, and the truth is because God has been using songs for a very long time as one of the greatest ways to express worship. Right from the first book in the Bible people sang and used instruments to exalt God. He commanded it.

Songs are a great way to connect the human heart to its Creator.

Unfortunately, the devil is also using music to do exactly the opposite. The devil is perverting the minds of millions and glorifying self, sex, money, power, and anything else to try and get people's focus off of God. Put only songs that please God through your ears and into your heart.

Also, begin to sing and use your voice to glorify God. Don't worry if you cannot sing very well.

God doesn't care about the quality of your voice, rather the heart behind the voice.

ACCELERATE TODAY

Read — Psalm 138:1-3

Think — What is holding you back from worshiping God with your whole heart?

Act — Don't be afraid to use your voice to bless God through singing.

GOD'S WAY

*Marriage is honorable among all, and
the bed undefiled; but fornicators and
adulterers God will judge.*
— Hebrews 13:4 (NKJV)

Sex!! That's right, God created it. He created it
so that we could enjoy our spouse in a way no one
else can. He created it so that we can have kids.
He created this awesome expression of love for
you to enjoy.

**The sad part is the devil is doing all he can to
destroy the value and sacredness of sex.**

The devil wants you to think it's okay to have
sex with someone you really love or that it's ok to
just get a quick thrill from anyone who will give it
to you.

You see, God put a boundary on sex until you
are married not to take away your fun but rather to
give you the greatest experience of sex possible.

Purity saves you from disobeying God, the heartbreak of giving yourself to someone you aren't married to, and the regret of not saving yourself for your bride/groom.

There are two ways you can go, God's way or the Devil's. The choice is yours.

ACCELERATE TODAY

Read — Colossians 3:5-6 (fornication means sex before marriage)

Think — What are some things you can do to ensure you go God's way?

Act — The bottom line is choose God's way! Save sex for marriage.

GREATEST GIFT

I urge you in the sight of God ... that you keep this commandment without spot, blameless until our Lord Jesus Christ's appearing.
— 1 Timothy 6:13-14 (NKJV)

Okay, be honest, how far would you like your future spouse to have gone physically with another person before you got married?

Would it be okay if they made out in the back seat of their parent's car? Would it be ok to you if they went further, and while they were making out, they started to take their clothes off?

What if you were able to stand outside the window of your future spouse's house and they are with their current significant other on the couch when no one is home? How far would you want them to go?

Would you be hurt if they went all the way and had sex?

The answer to all these questions is that it would definitely hurt! The point of all this is to show you the value of saving your virginity until you are married.

How amazing would it be to hear, "I have been waiting all my life to give this gift only to you." I think we all would like to hear those words.

My wife and I both were able to say those priceless words to each other on our wedding night.

It's up to you. Are you going to be able to give the greatest gift to your future spouse? I believe you can.

ACCELERATE TODAY

Read — 1 Corinthians 6:15-20

Think — What are some adjustments that you need to make to honor God in this area?

Act — You be the one that will be able to say to your spouse on your wedding night, "I've saved myself for you." At all cost protect your purity!

DECISION

Don't allow love to turn into lust, setting off a downhill slide into sexual promiscuity.
— Ephesians 5:3 (Message)

Purity is not something you just stumble into on accident. It is possibly the hardest thing for a teenager to hold on to. It is potentially the highest temptation on the peer pressure scale.

Sex is one of the greatest desires of the body. It is something that must be guarded with your whole life!

This whole issue of purity starts with making a decision.

You will not maintain your virginity (the greatest gift you could give) without making a decision and standing firm. I hear people who say, "Well, whatever happens, happens." Or, "We'll just see."

Anyone who takes this approach will fail, because purity is not something that comes easily. It takes making a decision and fighting for years to keep it.

The wait is worth it. Your future spouse is worth it. The decision is yours.

ACCELERATE TODAY

Read — Joshua 24:15

Think — What are some ways you can protect and maintain your virginity?

Act — Make a plan and a decision today towards purity.

WHO

The mouth of an immoral woman is a deep pit; those living under the Lord's displeasure will fall into it.
— Proverbs 22:14 (NLT)

If God is important to you, then your purity will be important to you as well. If purity is important to you, then today's topic is vital to your success in this area.

We are talking about who you are with. This is another big (Huge! Gigantic!) issue that is one of the greatest factors in keeping your virginity until you're married.

Who you choose to date will make or break you.

For example, if you date someone who does not have the same values that you have or does not believe in God, then you are setting yourself up for failure.

When someone is trying to find the right person, I always advise them to find someone who not only believes in God, but can lead them closer to Him.

Many people believe in a god; but few can push you closer to Him. I want to strongly advise you, in God's timing only, to involve yourself with a godly person who will lead you closer to God.

Settling for anything less will be planning to fail. It's all about who.

ACCELERATE TODAY

Read — Proverbs 2:15-18

Think — What are some characteristics of a godly girl/guy?

Act — Don't settle for anyone that is not God's best for you!

WHERE

Don't let your hearts stray away toward her (immoral girl). Don't wander down her wayward path.
— Proverbs 7:25 (NLT)

The sequel to yesterday's topic is, "where." Where are you going?

I think it is of utmost importance where you are with your boyfriend or girlfriend. Many people wonder how they got into the situation to lose their virginity. It is quite simple. They were with a person who doesn't lead them closer to Christ and they were alone when no one was home.

If you are alone with a godly person long enough, you have the potential to give into temptation.

I want to encourage you to guard the situations you put yourself in.

When I was a young teenager, I was drinking alcohol and smoking cigarettes. The only way I could quit was to stop going to the parties where this was happening.

I had to stop going over to certain friends' houses. I had to gain control of the "where." If you are going to make the right choice with purity, then you must guard the "where."

ACCELERATE TODAY

Read — Proverbs 7:21-27

Think — What are some situations you should avoid with the opposite sex (with virginity in mind)?

Act — Don't even get into situations that could lead to foreplay or sex until you are married.

DO OVER

How far has the LORD taken our sins from us? Farther than the distance from east to west!
— Psalms 103:12 (CEV)

Have you ever got into trouble with your parents, then one month, six months, or one year later it seems as if they forgot the whole thing? God is the same way with our mistakes.

If you have messed up with this whole purity issue, God will forgive you if you truly repent.

It is important to not just feel sorry, but turn from your former actions and ask God for forgiveness. This is true repentance.

If you made some mistakes and truly repent, God will forget about the whole thing. I am not advocating the thought process that says, "Do it first and say sorry later." The problem with that is you will still have the hurt and pain that comes from sinning and losing your virginity. I am not saying that with repentance comes no pain. Rather in God's eyes, it's a do-over; it's a second chance.

Here is a tip: When you think about the painful areas in your life, immediately replace the bad thoughts with something good. Colossians 3:2 says, "Set your mind on things above." This means when a bad thought comes in your mind, you must replace it with a scripture or a good thought.

So to those of you who have made a mistake, repent and take this opportunity to have a fresh start and a clean slate from God.

ACCELERATE TODAY

Read — Psalm 34:17-19

Think — How do these verses speak to your heart concerning past mistakes?

Act — 1. Think about all the ways you have messed up in this area. 2. Ask God to forgive you. 3. Change your behavior. 4. Stop thinking about your mistakes. Once God forgives, He forgets, so let it go.

PERSEVERANCE

Fight the good fight of faith and claim eternal life. — 1 Timothy 6:12 (CEV)

I can remember when my wife, Hannah, ran her first marathon. She did a fabulous job, and I was very proud of her. If she had gone out and tried to sprint the entire marathon, she would have never made it.

I think purity (the greatest gift) is similar in many ways to a marathon.

Let me make some comparisons. First, it was her training, her running foundation that she did for months to prepare that enabled her to finish. I believe that your foundation of purity is your morals and values. You will not achieve the satisfaction of completing a marathon without the foundation.

Secondly, along the entire 26.2 miles, there were people cheering the runners on. We can look to God and good friends to cheer us on and give us that extra boost we need to keep us going in the purity challenge.

Thirdly, Hannah kept before her the great honor and sense of accomplishment that the finish line would bring her. You must keep that before you as well. You must continue to think of the great honor and great gift that will be given to you and your spouse on your wedding day.

Keep these three steps on your mind as you strive to cross the finish line one day.

ACCELERATE TODAY

Read — 1 Corinthians 9:24-27

Think — In what ways can you apply perseverance into your life of purity?

Act — Take the necessary steps daily to win the purity prize!

IMPORTANCE

And I also say to you that you are Peter, and on this rock I will build My church, and the gates of Hades shall not prevail against it.
— Matthew 16:18 (NKJV)

God has created this great thing called church. Think about it. This is a place where you can go to get strengthened in God.

When you go to church, the Word is preached and God begins to deal with your heart.

Many times through the preaching of the Word, God speaks to you about areas in your life.

If you deal with these areas in your life, you will be strengthened in God. Other times, you go to church and you are carrying heavy weights and you feel discouraged.

This is a place that is designed to help you in your walk with the Lord. God's heart is that His people are not plagued with worry, heaviness, or depression. Life throws us many curve balls and the devil wants to push us to a sense of hopelessness.

Through worship, God can encourage your heart. Maybe a person at church says something to lift you up. God wants to use church as a way to strengthen you in Him and encourage your life.

ACCELERATE TODAY

Read — Luke 4:16

Think — How does this verse relate to consistency to church?

Act — Make the decision of consistently attending church. Make it non-negotiable in your life.

CONNECT

Your love for one another will prove to
the world that you are my disciples.
— John 13:35 (NLT)

So many teens today are crippled by the
people they spend time with. God wants you to
connect with other teens who want to accelerate
their walk with Him.

**He wants you to get around people that are
100% sold out to Him.**

This is another reason to be consistent in going
to church. God can use church as a way for you to
connect with other believers. You may feel like you
are alone in your convictions at school; however,
at church you are surrounded with tons of teens
that share your values.

Some people will say, "I can serve God on my
own, I don't need to go to church!"

This is false thinking. You will not be a strong effective Christian if you do not get connected to a local church. There are so many incredible, valuable benefits from church.

Make the decision to attend and stay committed to church for the rest of your life and connect with other believers.

ACCELERATE TODAY

Read — 1 Corinthians 11:17-22

Think — What does verse 22 mean to you?

Act — Make steps this week to truly connect with your local church and the people in it.

THE KEY

The key of the house of David I will lay on his shoulder; So he shall open, and no one shall shut; And he shall shut, and no one shall open.
— Isaiah 22:22 (NKJV)

Some people seem like they are in a car heading down a hill with no key in it and no steering. They are just flying down a hill going wherever the car decides to take them.

If they just put the key in the car and started it, it would unlock the power steering and the brakes.

Church can be the key to unlock a great and enjoyable, direction-filled life.

Church, many times, is the way God will direct you.

God uses pastors to give Godly direction that will ensure safety to your life. When you go to church, open your heart and mind to what God wants to speak to you every time you attend.

If you have an open heart and you actually do the things that the pastor challenges you with during the messages, you will unlock great blessings in your life.

ACCELERATE TODAY

Read — Revelation 3:20

Think — How can you apply this to your life?

Act — Open the door of church in your life.

BELONG

Consequently, you are no longer foreigners and aliens, but fellow citizens with God's people and members of God's household.
— Ephesians 2:19 (LB)

Church is not supposed to be a cold institution. It is not to be a place where you come to hear how bad of a person you are.

Rather, church has been designed by God to be a warm, loving, encouraging, challenging, and fun place to be. Better yet, it is a place to belong.

I am sure you have found this to be true in life that the most important thing is relationships. Everything revolves around relationships. You have friends, brothers, sisters, grandparents, a mom, a dad, a future spouse, a boss and a pastor, just to name a few.

The church is to be a place where you are surrounded with relationships with people who love God. The church is to be a loving family for you to connect to and embrace. Church is to be a place where you not only attend, but you feel a sense of belonging and ownership.

I want to encourage you to find a church that you can call home—a place that you enjoy attending, a place where there are godly people you can call family. God wants you to belong to His loving family and be connected to a church.

ACCELERATE TODAY

Read — Ephesians 2:19-22

Think — What is holding you back from connecting on a deeper level to your church?

Act — Focus this month on not just attending church, but finding a way to belong.

EMPTY

Our hope comes from God. May He fill you with joy and peace because of your trust in Him. May your hope grow stronger by the power of the Holy Spirit. — Romans 15:13 (NLV)

Empty is a word I was very familiar with. In high school, my hot rod Camaro was always on empty. I would run that thing until I had to basically coast into the gas station.

In college, I hit the wall. Yes, I ran out of gas on my way to class. I had to pay a hefty towing bill. If I had consistently gone to the gas station, there would not have been a problem.

Church is a lot like a gas station.

When our lives are on "E", we need to get filled up. The key is not to run on "E" and get charged with all kinds of life problems (towing fees).

A better way to live is to consistently go to church (the gas station) and get "topped off."

ACCELERATE TODAY

Read — Jeremiah 14:1-4

Think — Do you feel that your life's gas tank is full? Explain.

Act — Begin to fill your life with God's Word and a good church.

STRATEGY

A thief is only there to steal and kill and destroy. I came so they can have real and eternal life, more and better life than they ever dreamed of.
— John 10:10 (Message)

Could you imagine sports without strategy? The quarterback in football brings in the play and says, "Just go out there and do whatever you want."

Think about basketball with no pick and role, no plays, just whatever you want to do is fine.

It takes strategy to win. Without it, a team will fail miserably.

The devil has a strategy for you and it is laid out in John 10:10; he wants to "steal, kill, and destroy."

That is one of the reasons church is so important. The pastor lays out God's strategy to gain the things necessary to win in God' plan for your life.

Stay committed to church and committed to God's strategy for your life.

ACCELERATE TODAY

Read — Jeremiah 29:11-14

Think — Are you following God's plan for your life? Are you doing the things the pastor challenges you to do every week?

Act — Follow God's strategy and His plan for your life by doing what is talked about at church.

THE RIGHT CHURCH

In My Father's house are many mansions; if it were not so, I would have told you. I go to prepare a place for you. — John 14:2 (NKJV)

There are close to seven billion people on earth and no two are exactly alike. Even twins are different in small ways. It is the same thing with churches.

There are so many out there. How does a person choose a church or decide which one to attend?

I want you to know that God has already prepared a church for you.

I want to quickly give you a few pointers that will help you in life. You may move to different cities a few times and it's important to find the right church.

First, you must find a Bible-believing church that feeds you God's Word in a powerful way.

Second, you must find a church you can enjoy attending. Always remember it won't be exactly like the church you came from, and keep in mind no two churches are exactly alike.

Third, you must find a church that has people you want to befriend. It must be a place that can be like a family to you.

Finally, you must find a church where you can get involved and begin serving. Follow all four steps and you will always belong to a great church.

ACCELERATE TODAY

Read — Matthew 6:31-34

Think — How can verse 33 relate to finding a church?

Act — Make it your lifelong goal to always be in a great church no matter where you move.

EXPRESS

Therefore go and make disciples of all nations. — Matthew 28:19 (NIV)

The Bible says to make disciples of the entire world. What is a disciple?

It is a person who is a fully devoted follower of Christ.

God wants us to do something with our faith and that is to express it.

He did not create us to just eat all of this spiritual food and get spiritually constipated. He wants us to take what we know and help people with what we have been given.

One of the biggest mistakes teens can make is to not reach out to their friends with the Gospel. If you really know it and you believe it has changed your life, then why not share the greatest thing that ever happened to you.

I am challenging you to express your life in God to the world. The devil has plenty of people promoting false religions, Wicca, Satanism, and anything else anti-God. It's about time we stood up and expressed the truth!

ACCELERATE TODAY

Read — Matthew 28:16-20

Think — How will you apply this verse to your life?

Act — Start today to express God to people!

THE POWER OF ONE

Suppose one of you has a hundred sheep and loses one of them. Does he not leave the ninety-nine in the open country and go after the lost sheep until he finds it?
— Luke 15:4 (NIV)

A little boy was on the beach one sunny day and saw tens of thousands of starfish washed up on shore. They were lying helpless from the storm the previous day. The little boy began to pick up star after star, throwing them into the ocean.

An old man, seeing his efforts, came to him and said, "Why are you doing this? You are not going to make a difference."

The boy looked down, picked up a starfish, threw it in the ocean and said, "I made a difference for that one."

This is the power of one. It is when you focus on one person at a time.

The truth is you won't lead everyone you meet to Jesus, but if your eternity was at stake, wouldn't you want someone to care enough to pick you up and give you an opportunity?

This is why we must not think that we cannot make a difference. You can make a huge impact in this world by focusing on one.

ACCELERATE TODAY

Read — Luke 15:1-7

Think — What does this story illustrate to you?

Act — Make it your mission to impact ONE. (You impact one, who goes out and impacts one, they impact one ... and soon you have a lot of people living for God.)

LIMITLESS

I can do all things through Christ who strengthens me.
— Philippians 4:13 (NKJV)

The devil wants you to think you are useless, you can't make a difference, you can't do anything truly great, you won't make it, no one will like you, and no one will follow you. Why waste your time on something that won't work?

The devil is the father of lies. He is working overtime to get you to think that you can't make a difference.

But I want to tell you the truth: With God you are limitless!

Do not buy into the lie that you are nothing and you'll do nothing for God. You must dispel those thoughts, and start sowing different thoughts. You see, if you want to be average, sow average thoughts. If you want to be fearful, sow fearful thoughts. If you want to be intimidated, sow thoughts of intimidation.

The great question is what are you sowing into your heart and mind? I want to challenge you to put the truth in your mind.

Start filling your mind with what God can do. In school (with God), you are limitless in your potential to impact your friends!

ACCELERATE TODAY

Read — 1 John 3:1-3

Think — Did you know that you are God's kid? How can that change the way you act?

Act — Start believing that with God you truly are limitless.

GUTS

You cannot be my disciple unless you carry your own cross and come with me. — Luke 14:27 (CEV)

Do you have the guts to follow Christ? Do you have the guts to carry the cross? The cross symbolizes you living for Christ no matter how you feel.

Jesus was saying: Are you willing to leave it all behind? Do you care more about the meaningless stuff than about Me? Do you care more about how you look and feel than where people will spend eternity? Can you carry Me into your school?

Do you have the guts?

I hope you can answer yes to those questions. I want to see teens rise up and care more about what God thinks than what MTV thinks.

I want to see teens that are committed to the cause of Christ in a powerful way. I want to challenge you to stand up and stand out for God. He hung naked on the cross for you; won't you live for Him?

The question today is, do you have the guts to stand up for God?

ACCELERATE TODAY

Read — Luke 14:25-27

Think — What is it going to take for you to give your all to Christ and for you to have the guts to follow Him?

Act — Whatever your answer is for the above question ... do that!

FOCUS

Each morning everyone gathered as much as he needed, and when the sun grew hot, it melted away.
— Exodus 16:21 (NIV)

The sun is a powerful source of energy. Every hour the sun covers the earth with billions of kilowatts of energy. Yet with some sun-screen, you can bathe in the light of the sun for hours at a time.

An unfocused laser is a weak source of energy. However, when in focus, it takes a few watts of energy and focuses them in a specific stream of light. With its power you can drill a hole in a diamond or cut through steel.

In your relationship with God, it is important to focus. Focus when you are spending time with God. Focus when you are talking to your unsaved friends. Focus your impact to just a few people at a time. Focus your strategy to make a difference in your school.

I want to give you some vital information about focus:

Do Not Wait Any Longer — You must dispel the lie to procrastinate impacting others!

Do Not Have Wrong Priorities — Impacting people is the most important thing you could do!

Focus On The Power Of One — Put all your efforts on one person at a time.

Be Brave — You must dig down deep and act on what God says rather than how you feel.

ACCELERATE TODAY

Read — Haggai 1:1-8

Think — How can these verses apply focus?

Act — Focus on expressing God to people ... NOW!

URGENCY

I tell you, open your eyes and look at the fields! They are ripe for harvest.
— John 4:35 (NIV)

What if you knew that teens all across the world were dying of a terrible disease every day and you happened to have the cure? What would you do? Would you sit and do nothing while your peers suffered a horror, filled life only to know they will die any moment? Or would you do all you could to get the medicine to the world? This is an intense illustration, but this is happening spiritually.

Teens are in incredible pain and are desperate for what you have: a vibrant and fulfilling relationship with God.

Teens are dying every day without putting their faith in Christ. Your peers are going to hell if they don't turn their lives toward God.

You can do something about it. You have the cure. You can lead them to Christ. You can bring them to church. You can disciple them.

You can make the difference.

ACCELERATE TODAY

Read — John 4:34-38

Think — How does this illustrate the urgency of our time?

Act — Don't wait any longer, lives are at stake!

DON'T STOP HERE

*But you, man of God, flee from all this,
and pursue righteousness, godliness,
faith, love, endurance and gentleness.
Fight the good fight of the faith.*
— 1 Timothy 6:11-12 (NIV)

God is desperately looking for teenagers who will give Him everything—holding nothing back! This devotional, *Accelerate,* is not to be the finish line, rather the launching pad to daily connecting with God.

It is extremely vital to your faith in God that you commit to a life of acceleration towards God and His will for your life.

You cannot continue in a life without food, in a car without fuel, or in your walk with God without continualy filling up with devotions (Bible reading, prayer, worship, etc.). Friends, I desire more than anything that you continue in your growth process.

Remember what John 10:10 (NIV) says, "The thief comes only to steal, and kill, and destroy, I have come that they may have life, and have it to the full." God wants to give you an incredible life—unlike the devil.

How to have this full life is found in Matthew 6:33 (NKJV), "But seek first the kingdom of God and His righteousness, and all these things shall be added to you." This is so profound and so simple at the same time.

Put God first over everything in your life. This means give Him your time, your energy, your attitude, your relationships, and every thing else, and He will give you an abundant life.

ACCELERATE TODAY

Read — 1 Timothy 6:11-16

Think — How do these verses speak to your life?

Act — Make reading the Bible and praying a part of your everyday life from now on. Let this just be the start of a powerful life as a Christian. Fight the good fight of faith!

CONCLUSION

Congratulations!!!

You have completed the *Accelerate Devotional*. I want you to know I am proud of you! I am so excited to see you making God a priority.

I am sure that in these past eight weeks, God has grown in your life. I want to encourage you to keep going and keep growing in God.

A relationship with God is not a destination but a journey. Make spending time with God a part of your everyday life!

When you do this, you will enjoy a fulfilled life in Christ!

God bless,
Pastor Jake

COMMITMENT PRAYER

Dear God: Today I make the decision to follow You. I confess that You are God, and I will live for You. I believe You died on the cross and rose again to take away my sins. I give all of my sins to You now. I am choosing today to walk away from the things that do not please You. I am making a commitment to not only say I follow You, but to make the changes needed in my lifestyle so I can honor You. I will live a life set apart to You and You alone. In Jesus name, amen.

Congratulations on making the greatest decision of your life! Now connect with God on a daily basis.

NOTES

NOTES

NOTES

NOTES

For more info on Ignited Student Ministries,
go to:

IGNITED.ORG

For more books, resources, and info on
Jacob Ouellette go to: igniteme.cc